FLOURISH

Books by Dora Malech

Stet
Say So
Shore Ordered Ocean

FLOURISH

Dora Malech

Carnegie Mellon University Press
Pittsburgh 2020

Acknowledgments

Thanks to the editors of the following publications in which versions of these poems first appeared:

The Academy of American Poets Imagine Our Parks with Poems: "Catoctin Mountain Park"
The Academy of American Poets Poem-a-Day: "Each year"
Birmingham Poetry Review: "Caldo," "Little Offer"
Crazyhorse: "The Garden of Eloquence," "Personal Device"
Diode: "Aubade," "Minerals, Mine"
E-Verse Radio: "Neighborhood Watch"
Gulf Coast: "Parade"
The Hopkins Review: "Maximum Security," "Party Games"
The Iowa Review: "The Aquarium," "Flourish," "Notes Toward a Thank-You," "Working Order"
The Kenyon Review: "Running in Autumn"
Lana Turner: "Uprising"
Memorious: "For Eleza"
The Morning News: "Humility & Co."
New England Review: "As I gather"
The New Yorker: "Country Songs," "I Now Pronounce You," "To the You of Ten Years Ago, Now"
OmniVerse: "Euscorpius italicus"
Pangyrus: "America: That Feeling When," "Flight Map," "Lake Roland Park"
Pinwheel: "Late Lullaby," "*Portami il girasole . . . ,*" "Wind and Flags"
Plume: "Four Weeks," "Rats"
The Rumpus: "'Thousands are gathered outside the interior ministry . . .'"
The Shuffle Anthology: "The Gods Before Me"
Tampa Review: "Come Again"
Thermos: "Progress"
Versal: "With Distinction(s)"
Whiskey Island: "Dear Reader—," "Nominal Nocturne"

Thank you to the New York Public Library (National Poetry Month #PocketPoems) for publishing "Unconditional."

Thanks to the editors of the following anthologies for including these poems:

The Best American Poetry 2015 (Scribner, 2015; edited by Sherman Alexie and David Lehman): "Party Games"
I Know Now in Wonder: 25 Poems from the First 25 Years of the Civitella Ranieri Foundation (Persea Books, 2019; edited by Gabriel Fried and Dana Prescott): "Euscorpius italicus"
The New Census: An Anthology of Contemporary American Poetry (Rescue Press, 2013; edited by Kevin A. González and Lauren Shapiro): "Country Songs," "Humility & Co."
Poem-a-Day: 365 Poems for Every Occasion (ABRAMS, 2015; edited by the Academy of American Poets): "Each year"
Still Life with Poem: Contemporary Natures Mortes in Verse (Literary House Press, 2016; edited by Jehanne Dubrow and Lindsay Lusby): "Still Life"
Welcome to the Neighborhood: An Anthology of American Coexistence (Ohio University Press / Swallow Press, 2019; edited by Sarah Green): "Neighborhood Watch"

Library of Congress Control Number 2019953772
ISBN 978-0-88748-655-5
Copyright © 2020 by Dora Malech

for Kyle and Ada

Contents

I was pirouette and flourish,
I was filigree and flame.
How could I count my blessings
when I didn't know their names?

Back when everything was still to come,
luck leaked out everywhere.
I gave my promise to the world,
and the world followed me here.

—Rita Dove, "Testimonial"

Party Games

Might night right sight?
        —Andrew Joron

The first thing she did after we blindfolded her
and turned her in circles by her shoulders

was lunge
for where she thought her target hung

and hit tree trunk instead, with one strike
against it split the stick

in half to jagged dagger
in her

fists. The donkey gently swayed
within reach, barely grazed

and staring straight ahead with the conviction
inherent to its kind at the horizon

that a gaze
implies,

paper mane fluttering in the breeze of a near miss,
belly ballasted with melting chocolate kisses,

drawn grin belying its
thingness, rictus

of ritual and craft. She's grinning
too, and laughing, regaining

her balance,
planting her feet in a samurai stance.

She brandishes her splinter.
There's no harm in letting her

take another turn
without turning

her around again.
We think we know how this ends,

how good it feels to play at this,
violence and darkness,

the beast
that harbors something sweet.

Country Songs

My man does his crying on a fast horse.
I do my best dancing with strangers.
The child screams through the moment
of silent prayer, says, "It's a free country,"
says, "You and what army." You can't
trespass on a river, you're only in
the wrong when you step out of it
into this field. All false hopes translate
to *just beginnings.* There was no grace
of God. I went. No secret that the sun and
moon have always slept in separate beds.
Gives some steel, steals some time and
calls it "borrowed," bruises and calls it
"something blue." A red bird, a yellow bird,
not in the same hour's frame but close
enough for their color together to make
a kind of ringing. I thought he brought
the water from the spring but he's still
bringing. I delegated. My job is waiting.
Is drinking water. I'm learning to say
"It's a free country: this army, but not me."

Lake Roland Park

2016

Lilacs, mown grass, and the scent of my own soap rising from the back of my neck in the heat. The train downtown sighs by beyond the trees. A minute later, the train into the county looks the other way. Fancy all these flowers opening to mouth their truest names. In a notebook from last spring: *I don't want Robert E. Lee Park to be this pretty.* It's spring again now, earth's orchestra pit swelling into green strains, vernal reprise. In between, nominal reprieve: in the fall, executives announced the park's new name—which had long been the name of the reservoir itself, actually—at the groundbreaking for a new nature center, ceremonial photo opportunity with hard hats, shovels, smiles. Re-placed. I visited the park for the first time last May, the month after what the city calls, alternately, the riots, the unrest, the uprising. The bill to rename was introduced last summer, later, following the Charleston shooting. I can't hear it, but there's music all around me—literally. Everyone walking and jogging past wears headphones, earbuds. Imagine hooks and basslines, melodies unheard except for self-selecting audiences of one by one. Saying a thing's still slippery as the stones in the streambed of Roland Run. To say that we are listening is not to say that these are hearings, though there are hearings.

Uprising

after Pavese

Though his eyes are open, the dead man is not
all that moved by the stars. Body shaped to the fall,
he sprawls shattered. The evening grows colder, the living
are nowhere in sight. It was useless to try to keep track
of them all: who ran up his back stairs, who stumbled
into his neighbor's cellar, who walks through the fields
through the night and will throw himself down on the furrows
at dawn. Whose face, tomorrow, bent over its work,
will twist to its grief. Who will witness this, wordless.

Though the blood in his hair holds his head to the street,
he does not hold much stock in the stars. The living,
asleep, could each pass for the dead man. If two
lie together, the air between still holds a charge,
but only the air. Their bodies are done in, pressed against
the mattress as if to the stained stones. They're grateful
to die a little at night. Around each, a darkness coagulates.
The dead man alone lies out in the light. It's his right
not to admire the sky. It's his right to look down on its dark
uniform adorned with all those glittering revolutions.

America: That Feeling When

full of suicide Coke

each gush released
in turn into one
white plastic chalice's
open mouth aimed wide
at heaven's fluorescent
fixtures' flickers
to receive

the syrup's sacrament
wild for to hold its aspartame

the super in superfluous
gulp runneth over in
alchemical union

each perfect bubble
bursting to be

ascendant in the straw
that's stiff and red
as a child's drawing
of her father's
hardened artery

you pull off to the side
of a back road beyond a town
where flags wave two
different flavors of anger

flapping simulacra
of the stars above

here in the headlights'
stripes of light
bars of light

as what's in
wants out and can't
wait any longer
for the next gas station
convenience store

you unzip and squat

to darken gravel dust
to ink blot test over which

you bend closer
toward a glint that turns
out to be your

stream shining
a spent shell casing

Unconditional

If this black willow is calligraphy
then this white sky's an invitation
and requests the honor of your presence.
And you—will you attend?

I Now Pronounce You

Our friends are getting married in Duluth
in July, a city I had always pictured
in my mind's eye as ice in rivers, ice
in lakes, months of frozen glitter in shades
of the silver wedding invitation
held in place on my refrigerator
through my own cold months by a gift a child
once made for me, magnet glued to paper
with my name in pastel letters beneath
a flat-bottomed clear glass "gemstone," its strength
not quite enough to keep the heavy card stock
from slipping a fraction of an inch each time
I reached for milk or eggs, so by the time
summer arrived in earnest the betrothed
names were shimmering askew on level
with my shins and the vegetable crisper.

In the snap a winter back, the meteorologists
breathlessly proclaimed the city colder
than the surface of Mars as the temps dipped
double digits before wind chill.

                    Of course,
this factoid discounted Martian fluctuation
and that Manitobans have it harder.

I must admit that I was more thrown off
by the reality of Mars than of Minnesota,
as the Red Planet's, well, *redness*, and namesake
and dust storms left a fiery impression
on my early imagination that no
science could entirely revise.

We made a trip of it, drove from the coast,
collected mosquito bites like merit badges
in Michigan, New York, Ohio, Pennsylvania,
though not quite so alphabetically,
and camped on the shores of Superior
in a tent my boyfriend hadn't used for years,
which, when unfurled, contained a scrap of paper
with "I love you" from his hometown girlfriend,
who I had just met with her husband
for a drink or five on my part while passing
through said hometown.

                  I loved her for writing it,
I loved him for saving it, I loved the tent
for sheltering it and us, and I hate
myself for that other kind of dwelling
(on) in which nothing can live.

                  Clear water,
skipped stones, embers, stars.

                  In the morning,
stopping for gas station coffee, a pamphlet
in the spinning metal map rack on
identifying agates: translucence, banding,
heft, irregular fractures, and so on.

The pamphlet tempered expectations, warned
the reader not to try to find the store-bought
kind, which have been tumbled and polished
"to bring out their beauty."

                  Crumpled burger
wrappers, windows down, radio hits.

                              We arrived
in a sweltering Duluth of sweet flag, yarrow,
hyssop, clover, and sweated our way on a winding
walk before the evening's festivities,
up through the green of Enger Hill to see
the city from the tower.

                         In the garden
at the overlook, a replica,
presented by sister city Ohara,
of its "peace bell," taken by USS *Duluth* sailors,
then returned to Japan a decade later.

The oldest bell in Ohara, it had been destined
for wartime scrap, meant to melt, but spared.

For what reason was it never destroyed?

"For some reason it was never destroyed,"
the sign explains.

                         The wooden beam hung to sound
is wearing down, splintering edges and flat shine
of use. Pull back the beam and ring the bell.

Across the garden, two children look to the noise
that reaches them.

                    I was their age when
I learned my planets poorly and only slightly
older when I learned that sound is movement
and now the air and I are moved not only
by the knell itself but by the quiet commentary,
as a footnote in a smaller font, of rust on chains.

Late Lullaby

after Saba

Heat that fierce in October was rare.
You were my refrain, my heavy little pearl
back then. It was my job to fret over

the sun on your skin as we lay in the grass.
The stream, a hopeful playmate, gurgled, heard
but unseen. You asked about the sound. You asked

about everything then. I told you it was water
running louder after rain, which turned
over more questions: *from what? to where?*

My baby, I ask you now the same, it seems,
from far past where the stream unfurls
its white flag and gives itself up to the sea.

Ask me anything now and I'll answer. Come home.
I call to you from the place between wars
where men are back from their battles and little
girls have not yet been sent to their own.

"Thousands are gathered
outside the interior ministry . . ."

Bloody lullabies soothe the centuries.
Can't see the cradles for the tops of trees
but you know the rest: you can't rest, poor babies.

Keeper must feed the open mouth of *less than*,
promise sweet imminence lest its equation
flash its vast imbalance. All you can count on

is its truth is false. Tired of penance-
as-usual, its subjects take their chances,
lob bottles onto logic's premises,

throw garbage at the ever-guarded gates.
The grid goes down: the city burns now less
symmetrically. Volleys of rubber bullets,

real bullets, as cell phone videos
catch, like bloody butterflies, howls (souls?)
rising from the fallen. Chants of *life goes*

on until it doesn't, or so the slogans
sound mid-madness, around the salvoes' din.
This is test without constant, the red duration,

mothers hurling rock-a-byes: *my son died*
a hero. In an unspecified inside,
sanctum sanctorum, a kettle cries

for order or gives voice to its dissent,
rails against the status quo or against
chaos, depending on who's left.

Flight Map

after Mohammed El-Kurd, Lily Sickles, et al.

It's just an in-class exercise. I ask
each student to share a line so we can
collaborate, weave disparate histories
together. It's just for fun, I say—a phrase
that probably sounds less than convincing
coming from the teacher, but no one
protests. Heads bowed, they put their pens to paper.
Mohammed writes of a refugeed God.
I ask if he means simply refugee
or maybe exiled and he says no, he knows
what he means is refugeed. Lily writes
her hair into the nests of birds on two
continents. Genetics twists her locks
to echoes of the double helixes
that make a home of each of us. My mind
flits to the pair of doves I saw startled
from what they'd built in the eaves, how verbs aver
agency, and how one might find that nest
and say it had been abandoned. We're moving
on, I say. I have a lesson prepared
on the first-person plural. I hit the arrow
on the PowerPoint. Soon, our session
will adjourn and we'll board our respective
flights back to Newark or to Moscow
or Jerusalem. Doves live on every
continent except the frozen poles.
Here's where I try to convince you
that we'll always have each other's words,
the holy nest in what's said honestly.

Personal Device

Stare-gazing lap-glancing calls me all
the world's this rectangle set to the right

of shrimp fork, of steak knife, or a-knee like
a bleating, beeping baby, or yet more

precariously riding, like some trainer
in a Sea World orca act, the curved

black back of the toilet paper dispenser
in the public stall, or under sheets

and coverlet the body-built grotto lit
like alternate Waitomo glowworm caves

though boasting instead of constellations only
one enormous larva to its name.

Larva? Oh, let's say imago (like
the night is Jung) as this particular

specimen—*Arachnocampa luminosa*
(species of fungus gnat's syllable-bedazzled

stage name)—even almost grown glows on and on,
and then, the word (a stage) metamorphoses

into the word (as gate) and imago opens,
multiplies, becomes (Gods bless you, Latin)

imagines. *r u still there?* *sends up speech
bubbles* *i heart you*. Sure it smarts, but still

one can refresh, go for a scroll to clear
one's thread. All tongue tied to all thumbs trips

tremblesome, fumblesome, syntax mis-tapped
to sentiment's sediment, binary

slurry of zeroes and ones run to
x's and o's. Sighers, cipher. Rubble

up against. Send face by satellite
as text falls on the plane, the pane of dust

and scratch guard, case closed to hold contacts and
contacts close in case of impact. Never

alone here and never together, no rly
real here here to speak of though oh do we

speak of. Do we ever. Blind data charges
on, unlimited talk and text and talk

and text all u can eat-urge-grit—regurgitate,
swipe right, swipe leftoverautocorrect

angles, our better wreck tangles overhead,
invisible threads from the towers. *yr breaking*

up. yr breaking up? yr breaking up. An opposition
of thumbs, mis-tips my crows to bear in a murder

of crowd, trust as tryst, new coat's new cost, naked
named, take and tame, pride as price and time as

tune and knee as knew (I always liked that joint)
and lady last—what's the word I sd (sweet dreams)

sent in your ear as is in your war, denote,
demote and we were warmed as we were warned.

To quiet this body,

you must answer

my tendrilled craving.

    All I've ever wanted

was to kiss crevices, pry them open,

and flourish within dew-slick

hollows.

    How you mistake

my affection.

—Saeed Jones, "Kudzu"

Progress

Already failed resolution to spend less
time staring at squares, enrectangled up

in pixels, justified prose, polarized glass.
Data entry, no exit. Lint trap's just that.

Geometry that gestures toward itself
or not at all as in the inward wave

that in one culture simply greets and in
another draws one closer. Figures that

in my eyes it would beckon. Patterns swim
familiar but no one's there to take

an order and connecting the dots in
the vitreous humor makes a child's

stakeless game, a "now let's say" to made-up
playmate (and say that which we say it is

it is until we tire or some other
specter floats aview). Are you saying

you'd rather queue for keeps? Phantom limn
a charged perimeter? Wasting time

no matter but on what (all-important
distinction between phenomenon and

illusion). Mind's the former, sure, but great
stakes shaking no one's boughs' but mine but mine

tracing, racing, generating *orders,*
families, genera the likes of which

the earth has yawned and swallowed in its sleep.
How to take a turn to lean a body

through not to the execution? As if
we could adapt the course by tricking

out the question, force feed fattening
infinity on its own tail. Wakes into

passing scenery, a world of *ramifications*
blinking Darwinian landscaping escaping

into can't see for the topiary signing
line-on-line perpendicular, means ends.

Nominal Nocturne

Awkward additions
etched into benches,
scrawled onto stall walls,

bent on an *always*,
couplings meant
to cast a sure spell

over *forever and forever*
as if teenage talisman
or adolescent amulet

might overpower
oak roots and earthquakes,
city planners,

higher powers,
time, or even
the raccoon that jumped

from the dumpsters
the night before
the sidewalk's wet cement

set to sure
concrete, onto
and through

our initials and down
to the creek to wash
his hands of us.

Aubade

The sun's the only one of us
with a direct flight into Eastern Iowa.

What for us would be trespass
across farmers' land, hopping fences
and trampling crops, is the sun's
business, easement, egress.

The sun fords the Mississippi
and forges glittering tribute
of its little tributaries,
dazzling the windshields
on I-80 to a flashing river too.

Sun's rise razes, threshes, harvests,
planes plains to gold plate,
folds the fields into bright batter.

The Aquarium

My ticket paid and ripped, I wander under
water, through spines, speckles, snouts, suction cups.
Around one corner, I swallow abalones
whole. Around another, freed of my blood,
my bones, and brains, I find myself now blessed
with tentacles and toxins. Here, my left eye
migrates toward my right and I swim sideways.
There, because I fight when caught, I'm sought
for sport. Voyeur, I watch writ large two seahorses
making, if not love, at least new seahorses.
The video loops and loops and loops before
I let them go. Creatures like tumors, creatures
like sunspots, pulsing and drifting, I come
to at the lip of the "touch pool,"
an invitation to recall my hands.
Such pleasure to pry starfish painted by nature
to summon sunset from Plexiglas habitat
and imagine invasion renders a galaxy
for a moment urgent. I stand with others
poking snails now, nursing fantasies
of science and agency, moving creatures
from one corner of a glorified dish to another.
An older woman with an official lapel pin
shows a family the crab that decorates itself,
adorns its shell "like a lady might, or"—
playing to the crowd—"some gentlemen might
too." What in the wild would be wound of
other organisms—sponges, algae,
anemones—a crown to hide beneath,
a beauty born as byproduct of need,
here's a tangle of string, aesthetic accident
of instinct. Adjacent this pliable seascape
that merits the docent's discussion, other tanks.
In one, a baby shark, or shark writ small,

a shape I know to know as danger and
here what wonder right within my grasp,
form I feel I've come to touch, but when I lift
the lid and reach into the water there
erupts such a uniformed reprimand
I drop the lid, and not quite run, but "exit,"
the voice explaining in my wake "we had
an incident." This anecdote does not
surface into story, sure, no great scarring
to me nor shark nor tank nor institution,
my friends merely amused to find me hiding
by the otters, face pressed so close to my
reflection as to fog their seamless play.
But why so much to touch and the *don't touch*
right beside and signless? And why the rules
of the "touch pool" clear to everyone but me?
Wishing and wishing and never well enough
alone, outside, my eyes adjust, light left
upon an ocean too deep to fathom, light
right to shine a shallow fountain's change.

Echo:

      without
your code who

could radio news
of the execution?

Stutter utter
try I

echo:

      more
full of you

empty
the room

relinquishes
its furnishings

all entrance
entranced

to trial I'll
stand and

echo:

      you make
a song out

of obstruction
obstruction

out of song.
Inchoate

echo:

incite inside
and out your

origin again
begin in

a conspiracy
to sound.

Euscorpius italicus

You are not a killer but you play one
in my head. Tomorrow I'll leave the light on

for you since I think that isn't what
you want. Whatever it is that you want

must be small enough to fit within
your grasp. As if you are waiting in

the butcher's line and at a loss for words
you forever gesture overhead

this much. You have a lovely body.
It's sure to leave a mark. The shape won't do you

justice. This much we have in common. Let's get
out of here, but sideways. You go first.

Peter Piper Speaks and Spells

> "Selves—goes itself; *myself* it speaks and spells,
> Crying *Whát I dó is me: for that I came.*"
> —Gerard Manley Hopkins,
> "As Kingfishers Catch Fire"

Sour bite—

        be it or us.
    Past participle's
potent, see: past particles urged
cornichon-ward, jerked gherkin-ward as if
this were bread-and-butter of a stupid
joke. Seriously: can we un-this?
In this means: forever altered. Tongue twists
around a truth and tries it: here there's no
impermanent pickled, no vegetal reversals,
acetic rewind. I know, I know we must
not say (show). Laugh lashed to the mast
or cast in the deep, still can't mitigate
molecular level and steep away,
simply mollify the matter back
by sucking out the salt and vinegar
like venom. Darling, this is not that kind
of bite. So—

        so be it. Of
course run its ingredients' gradients,
after a time's immersion it emerges,
therapized, prized out of jar and into senses
rearranged across the tongue. Know the map's
a misconception. Silly schematic. Still, seek
it between back-of-the-myth of bitter
and tip-of-the-myth of sweet, splash, pinch, bit
to taste (blood), last laugh lathed lath (roof of the mouth)
erase a wraith (ghost of palate pathed) *mythed me,*
mythed me, now you—you know. A peck of what?
Be it or us,

                    sour bite,
          this tongue's for peppered
questions, pick of the letter, phonetic
frippery and urgent mission, art, lick,
ululate—articulate, and swallow
back—need, want, test, taunt,
pleasure. What it's like: salivatic
prophecene of just in kiss, experiment
conducted in the brain and brine, the raw
feels' aftertaste of call it almost-all-right
ever after, learn to love the pucker,
not "better" but lasting, something like cured.

Little Offer

For their kind, not a moment's doubt.
Unwavering devotees,
they never hesitate for lack
of ideology.

I know I'm neither first nor last
of my kind to admire
the way they aim at radiance
and take for their last pyre

the first open flame. A shadow
in shadows at their rite,
I am, as always, paid no mind,
as I illuminate

nothing. The wordless watchword must
closer, closer hum
from the heavy place in their weightless
bodies, the tripped alarm

silenced only as the scales fall
singed from their whole selves.
I'll wipe, again, their dust and ash
en masse from sills and shelves.

Misguided still means guided somewhere,
still *means*. Great Light,
I'll trade you all my lofty thoughts
(never aloft) and bright

ideas (always unlit) and credos,
edicts, theorems, tired
metaphors of moths-to-flames
for my pair of wings on fire.

Working Order

I stop midstride and cannot look away
from the ordinary

ticking of the multiverse,
senses

and simple machines that glow suspended
in September's light. I cannot attend

to my errands, errant, to think
I think of you and think

of you as I watch the sun slip
into something more and lick the horizon's lip

and bend in close
to burnish a bee going down on a hosta flower. Most

of my memory's relevant flash cards have fallen to flickers of trivia,
orphaned referents rendered arcana—

swarm cell, propolis, honey stomach, supersedure—
but still I remember

this creature to be innervated and that
in death it can still sting. I forget to what

end its venom lasts.
It and I lost in its act,

small gravity of its attention, patience stirring nectar,
I cannot say it gives the flower pleasure,

but I do believe there are no simple questions, senses, nor
machines. The afternoon's true task is elsewhere.

Running in Autumn

Here is where I saw a fox in August.
Now the whole trail blazes

red and rust
around the bend

as if the creature's color
shaped which season followed,

turned tail to all and fall and beyond
blushed to burning bush.

Smolder's second-order
must come next,

and when I turn the corner
into winter I'll remember

the shade of a mourning dove's
startle and ash in today's

foliate gold rush
as portent's pigment too.

A drop of mercury.
Of blood in water.

A small fire is still fire.
No telling what it can consume.

Rats

Sudden underfoot, this one cries back
echo of my outsized cartoon shriek.
In snow, I catch its passing by the tail's
naked drag, line drawn through the fallen
flakes between footprints, making not map
but mockery of any designs on following.
In summer, certain nights fall like ancient
rites as the rats appear en masse, frenzied
to orgy or worship. My planted patch
bared down to a brown square by morning,
I have heard mint and I have heard:
smoke bombs and a shovel and a shop vac
in reverse, steel wool and ground glass
mixed into concrete, snap traps, glue traps,
poison pellets, ammonia-soaked rags,
cat piss, a .22, anti-freeze, and something
called a Zapper, which takes four D batteries.
In the stark fluorescent light of labs,
they're how we've come to know
what's actually inside of us,
our pathways and our processes,
so why not in the this-is-not-a-test,
the dim and dirty actual of the world
as well? Loathing them's the only issue
upon which our city's residents can all
agree. The rat—that gnawer in the dark
whose open-rooted incisors grow endlessly
beveled, bedeviled, reviled, for whom satiety
is never-finished work, whose teeth without
relief would grow into a perfect spiral,
from whom we recoil without acknowledging
our own geometries of need and claim anathema
slips through our chain-link symmetries—cases

our foundations, traces where our walls meet
with the rub of its body's grease and each night
reveals itself in us as too close to the furthest
thing from what we think we want our want to be.

Catoctin Mountain Park

*He who thus considers things in their first growth and origin, whether
a state or anything else, will obtain the clearest view of them.*
                                    —Aristotle, *Politics* (trans. Benjamin Jowett)

Look out across
the ridges of trees
flushed red
as if holding
their breath
to blue distance,
a wager made
with the sky.

Look out over
the Appalachians'
eastern rampart,
then scrap the word for parts—
before, prepare, fortify—
to take possession of again.

On the road in, two wild
turkeys bustle off into
the brush.

Off the trail in wet leaves,
yellow eyes of a box turtle.

What I take
to be the stripes
of common shiner
in a riffle.

Alone, one might intone
whose woods, whose woods,
one might whisper
democratic vistas.

One might say
summit and *Summit*,
as elsewhere, but near,
are Aristotle's other
animals—political—
at fenced and guarded
leisure, though the wind

passes as it pleases,
and when it shakes
the trees, it is not
an agreement at all.

Maximum Security

What does the world look like to a Supermax inmate? Linderman
showed 60 Minutes photos of his former 7 x 12 foot cell, which
have a shower, a concrete bed, as well as a window with red
concrete bricks behind it. . . . Says former ADX inmate Garrett
Linderman, "The perfection of isolation, painted pretty."
—"Supermax," 60 Minutes, CBS News

Portland cement, slag cement,
fly ash, a coarse aggregate

like gravel limestone or granite,
a fine aggregate like sand, water,

accelerants without which the mixture
could take centuries to truly

cure. Pigments with which the gray
matrix mimics brick. More water

increases workability,
less water, strength. The consistency

of a batch is measured by its slump.
Too much water results in bleeding.

The Romans added horsehair to reduce
cracks while hardening and added

blood to resist frost. All concrete
cracks somewhat. Steel bars or mesh

inside to reinforce. All pigments
reflect and absorb light's wavelengths

selectively to make color,
meaning of course that color depends

upon its source of light. Sunlight,
say, or searchlight. Pigmented concrete's

known to fade. Impermanent pigments
are called fugitive. Stare

at the red wall past a white wall. Now
close your eyes and the red wall's gone

green. Is this the garden we were
promised? Or the quiet forest, the one

where the trees fall all over each
other without a sound? I am not

one who can presume that anyone
pretends so well. No sun or moon

or filament or dream can catalyze
concrete to portent, make "take warning"

or "delight." I am not
one who can presume that anyone

can blur his eyes until they run
where middle distance makes its great

escape, believing what he sees is
a red sky, an augury of anything.

Minerals, Mine

> *In 2010, Congress passed the Dodd-Frank Act, which directs the Commission to issue rules requiring certain companies to disclose their use of conflict minerals if those minerals are "necessary to the functionality or production of a product" manufactured by those companies. Under the Act, those minerals include tantalum, tin, gold or tungsten.*
>
> —U.S. Securities and Exchange Commission

Tantalum, tin, tungsten, gold—

the empire's not-so-new attire's
dead man walking contradiction

sheer as starlet's ceremony
garb and red as the red carpet

flowing past her red-soled shoes,
a rivulet bisecting silver

screen, infusing plasma in our
darkened rooms beyond which sources

run unclear as that coy lady's
age whose years elide untold—

tantalum, tin, tungsten, gold.

Invisible supply chain mail
returned to senseless sender site

unseen, all that we can't touch
inside the screen in light of luxury

and lap of Lethe's waters leaving
only tracers, trails, and ghosting

vision, devices' divisive
origin stories all but obscured,

blood and sorrow, a row of hands
but not applause remains, remains

unrevealed (un rêve à LED)
ore mined out of mind or ore—

and here I pause to check missed calls,
to take a break (refrain—refraindre

from refringere—break) and watch
old news unfold in pickaxes, pixels,

tantalum, tin, tungsten, gold—

again, refrain, and break, again—

tantalum, tin, tungsten, gold.

With Distinction(s)

pasts' *pssts* : I repeat myselves
demotic motes : desacralized dreamscape
no nest-ness : debutante's endless escalations and détentes
dumb pendulum swung : took a header
rendered whomever : streaming seamlessly
haptic hat trick : we grasps at asps
makeshiftless currency : afield of a billion trillium
century at inattention : horizon's orison
commuted sentience : gentians' sleepy sentry
née anon : paramour's parameters
whose razed roses raised : prophylactic mandala
condescending a staircase : analysand's ampersands
and let me tell you a little story : about information all
in a de rigueur row : adapted the platform
brief denied backchannel : word into edgewised up
table upon table of discontents : good golem gets its aleph
for keeps : that's not true about rights
I mist you : thou dust
remade is re-minded : kitty-corner cubicle
carpal tunnel vision neck crick : here's looking and looking
no quick fix except : stammering sidle saddled
fall out of : headlong life long-
lapsed synapses : it was always the difference between
felt up and touched up

Working close, alone in the blond arena,
Flourish my cape, the cloth on the camera.
For women learn to be a holy show.

I'll tell you where I've been, not what I am:

—Carolyn Kizer, "Where I've Been All
My Life"

Come Again

These are the runes that ruin me, today's telling typos:
Heavy police pretense. Thank you for your corporation.

Jane invents the word *era-ist* for those of us
who discriminate against the past. Careful, it's not erased.

The birds persist in rapid-fire accusation: *Isn't-it-so? Isn't-it-so?*
then feign ignorance in response, slurred syllable made two: *Me-e? Me-e?*

The waitress apologizes, *Sir, there's no syrup, so so sorry, Sir.*

Trying to get from here to there, familiar with Flower,
one has to ask: *is Hope a one-way street?*

A man once promised to meet me at Liberty, but now's not at it.

Did we install the filter backward?
An errant arrow faces the wall like a dunce.

I make: my bed, peace with, amends, and light of—sure.

Epistolary too's a kind of aim, a game like pool in which you can't
just shoot, must point to the greener pasture's pocket first.

On the patio, the woman on her second wine carafe
screws up her courage to ask the waiter: *what are legs?*

Across the Missouri border:
CHEAP SMOKES FIREWORKS WHISKEY WORMS.

At Bruno's, *I'll have another one* slurs to *I'll have an urn.*

Inking inklings in the crossword, I pen a cramped crescent in
after I mis-guess the answer for *hole-making tool*:

It's *auger*, not *luger*. I'm off one letter. I'm off again.

Each year

                    I snap the twig to try to trap
the springing and I relearn the same lesson.
You cannot make a keepsake of this season.
Your heart's not the source of that sort of sap,
lacks what it takes to fuel, rejects the graft,
though for a moment it's your guilty fist
that's flowering. You're no good host to this
extremity that points now, broken, back at
the dirt as if to ask *are we there yet.*
You flatter this small turn tip of a larger
book of matches that can't refuse its end,
re-fuse itself, un-flare. Sure. Now forget
again. Here's a new green vein, another
clutch to take, give, a handful of seconds.

The Gods Before Me

The drawing teacher taught us
                              not to find
our outline and then fill ourselves in
                                        not
to start with the pupils and spiral outward
from there
              not
                of course
                              to trace
                                        under
any circumstances
                    and instead
to focus everywhere at once
                              to train
our eyes on *everywhere at once*
                                but now

                              that I'm in a room where I can be sure
                                no one will look over my shoulder

                                I plan to draw as poorly as I please
                              and let my horizon and all its clutter
                              creep completely from the right in one
                                  messy migration to keep my clumsy
                              left hand and its pencil from smearing
                              the fundament and firmament to keep
                              my quite inconsequential sun peering
                                  clearly over a hill's slight shoulder
                          and farther off into the blind unadorned.

Forced Perspective

Who says I shouldn't get close to the camera
and open my mouth around the scene, catch
my monster face in midchomp or midscream,
compel the poor machine to focus on
my pores and blur the horizon behind?
My antics fill the frame like it's a clown car,
pinkie hooked in cheek to act the catch
just so, unflattering angler obscuring
the punch line of a *Fishing By Permission Only*
sign. Snapshot, I am the captain of this
caption, gone down with the viewership.
In the article about the famous female poet
the reviewer bandied *bleary*, writing it's often
as if she's just noticed something interesting
and motioned the reader over, only to stand
in his light, blocking his view with her own viewing.
I remember a frisson at first reading,
followed by that falling feeling that comes
on seeing someone else get served a slight,
realizing your ration's from the same pot.
Better now to assume it was the periodical's
house style choice to render the reader
henpecked as *he*, or take it personally?
Among my mentors (men), one told me
I was *just trying to crack myself up* in my poems,
or *cheer myself up*, if I might aspire
to more than a bit part in the tragedy.
Another made me flail to pass the test
of his *what do you <u>want</u> me to say about these?*
before he'd address my drafts. Why am I
telling you this? *No admissions against*
interest, my mother always says. Save face.

And yet—this is no admission. Watch me
prop that Pisan campanile with a single palm.
See how it takes me just one foregrounded
finger to put the Eiffel Tower in its place.

Still Life

These are the brushes that I say I use
to paint, when in fact they are the brushes
I used to use. It seems these days they refuse
blues' glints, rays, blaze, dove grays, and sunset flushes—

unconsummated sight unseen, eyes' hues
and cries renounced in hibernation—or such is
my excuse, as if these *things* can choose
to love, not love the world, and this hush is

not a winter of my making. How might
I reseason palette's palliative,
focus my gaze to take to heart my flight
of—shade, stroke, swash, line—anodynes? Eyes give

chase across my table-scape to light
on trinkets from once-friends, an empty sieve
for loose tea, feathers once flown and a bright
lacquered bird, a glass unicorn's once shiv-

sharp horn broken to mere glass horse, a few
stones from a coast I miss, a few used matches,
deer's tooth, geode, to-do lists un-struck-through
indefinitely, those accusing brushes,

free pens from doctors, a stapler's open bite,
and beyond, the windowsill's relative
order, gray-green fireworks of epiphyte
which, despite my best neglect, still live.

To the You of Ten Years Ago, Now

Never fear. I know the difference between
arteries and ardor, arbor and treed,
my bower and a weak-kneed need, a harbor
where one might moor tonight and a port worth
the oars' effort to come ashore for, a bit
part and the serpent's gravid apple. I won't
flatter myself first or lasting, or
presume to fast and feint a martyr, making
mockery of sacrifice, fatten
for some sweet slaughter. I must believe that I'm
not on your mind. On your body? Sure.
That said, your body has a few ideas
so bright that we might meet some night and render
a dark room light as the last day before
the world ends, that doom that was supposed to dawn
today, but by now, hours worn on and in,
we know there's no such luxury as fine
as that finality for now. For now,
at least, I'll have to kiss apocalypse
goodbye, resign myself to this more mundane
pain, the solace of the solstice, year's
earliest sunset and its longest night.
I try to catch that fade of color with,
without a flash. Both tries prove terrible.
The horizon smudges up against the sky's blur
like a child's heavy-handed landscape
and inept erasure. They'll have to do.
The pictures that I have of you will never
do you justice either, neither a camera's
snap nor some synaptic crackle long
elapsed can come remotely close to holding
you. How else would you have it? You need
never fear. I need you, but I only need you
where you are: there, never far, never near.

Humility & Co.

I left a little cake, a little note:
I'm sorry if I threw up on your Christmas.
Dear, you can call it catharsis, it's still
bad manners. As if it were possible
to cancel all the flux inside, one wakes,
a levitating magnet. This is physics,
friends: the law of tell-you-when-you're-older,
ends that justify a good cry on
an iffy shoulder in the interregnum.
Wire-mother loves to cuddle the holidays
away, swings her dinner bell and waits
for drooling. Her "here there be" is
the crossroads of psychosis and bad
grammar where "someone" becomes "they"
and no one cares anymore. I guess she
fears what she sees as inexact, assumes
the loss or at the very least a lack of basics.
We can agree on take a penny, leave a penny.
On it's been a pleasure. On close the door
gently and please hit the hall light when
you leave. One option is embrace
stasis, and yet some days the heart's
this dirty, matted mutt trembling at the feet
of the family passing time between trains
in the station café: "Look, Mom! It wants
something!" Let's walk down and watch them
fire the cannon. Let's see if they're still putting
the puppet show on in this rain.

Caldo

I wished for strength
on the chatter of *spiccioli*
small change and stems tied

in knots by a tongue
in a mouth too shy to try
to assay aloud in lively company

submerged in language still
travel-logged and catching
only lonely pretty pieces

a piece of fish a piece of peach
di pesca like beach glass instead of
the bottle's rhetorical entirety

bright conjugated schools of verbs
passed through ripped nets
with scales unscathed

I asked myself what animal
could ever really carry
me to termini except perhaps

this wounded one
anima limping last letter lopped
off can't climb the stairs can't

say its name or any
as I would know it so
it sounded so

until all about then felt
parlor's pallid parlance
flush sudden prestidigitation

tripped the lexical kaleidoscope
spun most marvelously
mutable babble

capello cappella
hat turned to chapel
hour spun gold *ora oro*

mela miele mille
apple rendered honey
honey making a thousand

straws I grasped to hear
banners of silk at stake
and all this made to make

its own order
as even when I heard
word of word for without

senza began to sound
like sense vertiginous
verity witnessed

sorcio a mouse drop
from a palm a poem
added an accident

and saw the letter
to be good measure
as what fell from grasp

then was a glimpse *scorcio*
view was sure was true as I
could feel it happening to me

free and not free
sublime parole *parole*
fled the party

for as my friend once shamed
himself by saying to the butcher
I can't see without my mirrors

had to catch my
hatch my found
a washroom in which

to scald myself
on the certainty
of someone else's C

Dear Reader—

I miss the smell of my skinned knee the summer
I pulled my whole self alone under the covers
and willed it to heal. By *it* I mean *insert*
unclear antecedent here, by *here*
I mean *there*, by *there* I mean *above* but
also of course *inside*, as in my *inside*
voice, which is the voice I use when you're sleeping
so as not to wake you from slumber's muted
palette into the day's oh-so-color,
or rather, the voice I use when I pretend
you're here with me and you and I just had
a fight over whether art matters and you make
like your finger's a dagger you pull across
your throat to end it all and I make like
my pointer's a barrel and my middle's a trigger
and I hold the weapon up to my temple and fire
complete with kickback and brain-blast action
as illustrated by my other hand's explosion
and you gag louder; I thought *I can't put that in here*,
meaning *my knee, my poem*, but then your voice
in my head said *that's what she said*, and I knew
that we were still in this together and that I could
never have shared this with anyone but you.

The Garden of Eloquence

*. . . conteyning the figures of grammer and rhetorick, from
whence may bee gathered all manner of flowers, coulors,
ornaments, exornations, formes, and fashions of speech, very
profitable for all those that be studious . . .*
                    —Henry Peacham, 1577

From the sences

of the body.
From the sight—

inside the book

I picked across
blackletter script

sooner seen

through antique eyes,
view less bloomed

than brambled as I

stumbled under
lavish versals'

shadows, *no*

certaynty gathered,
a bitter kinde

of mocke, when,

stuck on the past
typeface's s's

stretched, as f's,

as every *aster*
ever *after,*

lest, left, last, laft,

hast, haft, chased, chafed,
my mispercept

leapt to *reach*

above the truth
and teach mistake

as precept, no

origins
except, accept—

from the fences

of the body.
From the fight.

Portami il girasole . . .

after Montale

Bring me a sunflower so I can plug its roots into
the socket of my salt-scorched coast. All day
let it display the little burning of its face, turn to
the sky that flashes back blue takes on its anxiety.

Darkening things still stretch toward what is
bright, bodies overreach, bleed into a wash of tints
and shades, pigments that, synesthetic, rinse
into musics. Unwitting, we wished. What luck it is

to vanish. Pluck up the petalled pinwheel that conducts
the gold crescendo of hours into haze, the surge no
orchestra can follow. Three hundred thousand volts into
the vault. Bring me the sunflower, crazy with light.

Parade

after a postcard from Special Collections,
University of Houston Libraries

Dear, when we say centuries *turn*, we don't mean midnights, merely. Picture instead, perhaps, an era's shift more like some lumbering march-past float might take a corner. Then see here how our postcard captures such a subject, captions a swatch of blue in the upper left as follows: THE WORLD FAMOUS RED HEADED WIDOWS OF HOUSTON, TEXAS, IN FRONT OF THE HOME OF THEIR CREATOR, THE HOUSTON POST. Our creator? Here, *The Houston Post*'s synecdoche for George Bailey, but not *that* George Bailey, silly. Here in this rectangle, it's 1909, our century's still turning like we said, and Jimmy Stewart's just a baby barely born in Pennsylvania. *This* Colonel George M. Bailey is an editorialist for our aforementioned paper. Our paragrapher extraordinaire, he's busy branding his city, boasting us—muses of Heavenly Houston—into being. And our husbands? That's the joke—don't cry for us! Our sobriquet means that we're mostly married to the fourth estate. Ours is a hometown wink lost to time's translation. You'll have to trust us that it's clever. Here atop our mobile wedding cake, our faces blur, pink ink beneath our bright bouffants, above our high-collared black dresses. The patient pony pulling our platform pauses for the picture. Now flip the frame over to see the blank space behind us where some stranger might have written what he wished—town square forever unconsummated by correspondence, the usual phatic script—the paper's lignin aged to liver spots, the years' asemic writ. Up the side: PUBLISHED BY S. H. KRESS & CO. Yes, *that* Kress but remember, the lunch counter sit-ins of Nashville, Greensboro, Baton Rouge are still decades later. For now, it's business as usual, just the chain of five and dime stores, purveyor of stationery and notions. (When your world's a postcard, all notions are stationary, and the crowd's forever gathered on the balustrade to better glimpse your pyre-colored hair.) What selling and what celebrating our procession promises! Here, our moment's yours in two dimensions for a cent—*The Houston Post* of Houston Past's Red Headed Widows—something someone said to smile and say we are.

As
though our garden
could be one bean
and we'd rejoice if
it flourishes, as
though one bean
could nourish us.

—Kay Ryan, "The Best of It"

For Eleza

The succulents you plucked
for me from the abundance
of your yard and nested
in a blue butter cookie tin
with shells and stones
for me to take home
across time zones
coast to coast not only
rooted in their indoor
plot of terracotta here
in Baltimore but thrive
so wildly I have to cut
them back and even then
new white pink roots
and fat green baby fingers
pull themselves up and out
to propagate from the now
calloused ends of once
raw leaves and stems

which is to say thank-you.
I have tried to let this growth
exist a welcome fact
without forcing it back
at you as figure of
though you thrive riven too.
I have watched you dive
through waves to disappear
and then emerge out past
the breaking with a smile
and your hair in tangles
and even this image
of your actual figure need
not stand as figure either

just exist in fact of memory
as do the grains of sand
and bonfire smoke
still clinging to my clothes
when I unpack.

I have smoothed plaster
onto your pregnant belly
and watched as it set to hold
your shape the week before
your first daughter entered
the world through you.
You know all this already
but a litany of *remember when*
is the closest that I can approach
to prayer or spell as if words
could conjure your mother
or husband alive again with you.
We say *lifelong* to mean *always*
 but both shift like shorelines.
I used to believe in believing
and thought that if life hurt
it meant to trust that it was
working like rubbing alcohol
and all strong medicine.

That was before I knew you
or anything. In the past's present
you are making a mobile
of driftwood. Long after
your daughters look through
its slow turning the shadows
it throws still make sense
of a relationship with light.

Neighborhood Watch

My back porch looks out on an alley
into which a neighbor's consumptive sump pump
coughs violently and sporadically at all hours.

Sometimes I pretend the alley's leaves and litter
stand in for Pharoah's army, rendering the effluence
a dramatic player in a Biblical tableau.

Sometimes I fancy the flow some misguided New Age appropriation,
a feng shui fountain—and at the north end of my home, no less—curative
imbuing elemental prosperity, blessing my "career and life path area."

Sometimes taking the trash out in the dark quiet of a Monday night,
I screech and leap at the sudden gush, my reflexes puppeteering me,
B-movie heroine to the drain pipe's poltergeist.

I seethe a little as I nod a greeting to my neighbor
on the rare occasions when he shuffles past, stepping
over his brown-green scum stream as he exits my scene stage left.

We engaged in the perfunctory name exchange when I moved in
years ago, but in disuse, those hinges between us rusted shut.
Mr. Whomever—I can't remember. Perhaps I should consider

my stage left as his stage right, and in his theatre, the conflict is
my music, my laughter, my little dog's loud demands, my penchant
for pantslessness and open windows on warm nights.

Can I call this a watershed and thus trace thoughts and follow
feelings sourceward? Try to imagine his basement,
how wet it must be to warrant such round-the-clock diligence.

Try to imagine our whole block is one leaky boat
and he's the only one bailing, not standoffish
as he seems, but just immersed

in the thankless necessary work, only emerging on occasion
to take the air and remind himself that we're worth saving,
though he's the only one who seems to see the sea.

Notes Toward a Thank-You

Illegible ledger scrawled on the walls
of the mind's interior, unseen but seen *to*

and shaping as a place makes nexus
of the prior and the next,

its grace suspended in an amber
chamber, praises pressed as flowers

in chapters of rising action and falling,
expressed in the rising and falling

of the sleeping chest after endurance—
you can have the rest—or ink if we take

card stock manners over mind
and think to thank indelible.

Excess can be gratitude, as can
restraint. I left some

pastry on your porch. I left
some flowers in a former marinara jar.

I don't expect you to keep them forever.
I don't expect them to keep. I took

a roadside spectrum out of context,
ditch lilies whose unfurling says:

can't help ourselves from blooming
so please help yourselves

to us too. This bursting *at* as if all else
were seams, field sown to open,

reveling in its unraveling.
Earlier I felt past try, I felt flow errs,

but routine is a route in—I stand by it.
Tangled in lines rapt in the net,

votive's motive meaning now's avowal,
and the dough risen *to* as if today

were the occasion, something
still sweeter at its center.

Wind and Flags

after Montale

The gust that hoisted the salt scent
from the sea unfurled over
the valleys' switchbacks down
the garden's hidden path to where
a bully in love it tousled your hair
to a crown of tangles and later
up the steep steps to the square
plastered your dress to you then
elbowed the men in the café chairs
and at night an angry drunk sent
trash bins flying slammed doors
rattled shoved started a fight
between the docked boats
that same so difficult invisible
resistance now that you're gone
for sure has sober returned shamed
slinks into the garden to rock
your absence in the hammock
strung between the cedars.
The waves will never throw
the bones not paint their forebear's
portraits on the sand nor sign
the waterline in quite the same way
twice and we are saved as such.
Our fable would rip itself
to pieces if we ever found again
ourselves together in the wind.
The grains the glass metes out
shape down the coast little tries
at villages barnacles clinging
to the hulls of the hills dressed
for a saint's day in their best
bunting and ships' pennants
strung across the narrow streets

bright fluttering bits and tatters
hauled home as a child might
drag weeds and shell shards
back up from the shore proof
that a bright place he remembers
exists or existed. I surface
with a start to sunlight to see
those to whom the world
gives nothing give thanks.

As I gather

                    my hair back from my face,
I smooth at the temples with my palms but
then move down the length to end in a fist,
which I hold for a moment as I pull
to cull

            casually the errant strand
broken by the elastic band, or cull
by more unsettling clump the throwaway
flyaways.

            On my way to a lunch date
or a meeting, I surreptitiously drop
the telogenic tangle on the sidewalk
or shake it off

                        my hand and out the window
of the moving car before it can cling
to my shoulders like bedraggled epaulettes
conveying not military authority but frazzled
absent-mindedness or worse (depression?
vitamin deficiency? pregnancy?).

The strands scrawl the sink in long lines
like the mark the pissed-off kid keyed into
automotive paint, or like my doctor's signature
reduced from letters' legibility
to the P-wave of an EKG
after years of autopilot signing scripts,
or like the creeping internodes of stolons
in my garden.

The billboard over
Chestnut Street features a new campaign,
a bottle of shampoo daydreaming
of a second life: "I want to be
a hairbrush. Recycle me."

                              At another corner:
"I used to be a plastic bottle. Now I
travel the world."

              At happy hour
I glance from birds emboldened underfoot
by bits of tortilla chips fallen on the patio,
to the heads of my neighborhood friends,
and back again, and picture Thea, Khaliah,
and Cassie's hair entwined in mine and cradling
some speckled eggs.

                    I know I can't be entirely
alone in hoping birds will use our hair
to build their nests, weave it through the twigs
and straw and string and make of us some
habitable dwelling, or rather, if birds use
our hair to build their nests, I know I can't
be entirely alone.

              All I want
is some part of me to be useful, or
beautiful, or both (the best of worlds),
and I'll take it as it comes, even in leavings
and only in avian reverie, a hypothetical
treetop bower I'll never see.

When my ex and I
parted ways, we each left the other with a gift.

He kept the drawings I had made in our shared
time and space, strands of color tangling
to form.

I kept the nest he found by the corral,
woven from the coarse lengths of manes and tails.
I like to imagine a whole herd wound
round and into one, an animal vortex,
which, if given the opportunity,
could run

faster and farther than I can even
imagine my body taking me.

I scour
the bathroom, if sometimes less than diligently.

My husband does his share.

This morning,
he asked if I noticed he had cleaned
the mirrors.

What hair that gathers on
the chrome lotus pod of the bathtub drain
swirls to take its shape, a wet rosette.

I swipe it up.

Still, our showers tend to end
in standing water, always a clog farther
down inside the pipe eventually.

The culprit's always mine.

Is me.

I check myself in the unmarred mirrors,
repin what inevitably flies free.

Gratitude

       that one expends expands,
glass less full than effervescent, shook spray
making rainbows, rainbows making certain
skies promise, promise making and remaking
itself imperfectly each day as a note
coaxed from the glass's lip, sip or spill
to shift the pitch and sing out what is missing

On the fence

                    thick-tangled with morning glories,
all of which have curled back in on themselves
by now, midafternoon, one September
clematis blooms like the little girl who fights
sleep at naptime, refuses to lie down
and close her eyes beside her friends in silence.
All right, clematis. I'll tell you one more story.

Four Weeks

Conscripted cells tunnel slip roads
through lining, making space apace
for blood to shush and nourish. I hear
the work's begun in earnest. I hear
you've got a primitive streak,
so to speak, like your mother.
My micro-morsel, does it feel more
seam or fin to you, this fine line
of yours winking dorsal in the still
still waters? In other words, are you
my plaything or my predator?
I know—it's too early now
to say, and certainly to speak
to you. Flickering ember's false
etymology glows in every
embryo, but even the fact
of your future's still unclear, less
crystal ball, more drifting snow
globe flake, a weather of whether
and maybe. So far, so far, as *mine*
divides *in me*. See you later,
party favor. Blip, meet radar,
sure, but it's all blasts building
on a toy horn, unless—shh.
You're just a guess. No symptoms
yet except this pesky tenderness.

Flourish

Clematis, sweet pea, sweet alyssum,
sweet asylum,

adornment's adamant
heaven scent

to bed an arbor's
ardor,

trellis's
yes this

reaching toward
its own reward,

sweet re-aching might redeem
what seems

a frail unfurling to refuge
instead, re-fugue

played in contrapuntal context
shows some pragmatist's *thanks*

thriving
not only as noun and verb, but *stem*, climbing

aster and hydrangea, honeysuckle,
wisteria, twine and tendril

reaching skyward
toward

as if to pick
a warden's lock,

as if jazz hands, spirit fingers,
fireworks, as our shared shards glitter

on this floodlit stage left empty and the river rising like ovation
out of whose rush and rake and raze and refuse grows again

these petals, pleats, sequins,
pirouettes, curtsies and klieg-eyed bowers, surefired lines

run to sun's stunning
statement piece, peals on which an hour slips under

the higher wire
and over

the big top we make
of what's at stake,

tensile
tendrils

corkscrewing up to pour more sunlight,
celebrate

the act
we make of the temporary fact of us.

Thanks to the Baker Artist Awards and the Greater Baltimore Cultural Alliance for a Mary Sawyers Baker Prize; the Amy Clampitt Fund and the Berkshire Taconic Community Foundation for an Amy Clampitt Residency Award; the Poetry Foundation, Don Share, and Christian Wiman for a Ruth Lilly Poetry Fellowship; the Civitella Ranieri Foundation and Dana Prescott for a Writing Residency Fellowship; Johns Hopkins University for a Catalyst Award; the Academy of American Poets for commissioning "Catoctin Mountain Park" for the Imagine Our Parks with Poems project; The Englert Theatre, Andre Perry, and Katie Roche for commissioning "Flourish," "Gratitude," and "Notes Toward a Thank-You"; *Gulf Coast* and Erika Jo Brown for commissioning "Parade" for "The Archive Issue"; Kira Wisniewski and Dillon Babington for including "Peter Piper Speaks and Spells" in the "Call + Response V" multimedia collaboration; and The International Writing Program, Christopher Merrill, Nate Brown, Ashley Davidson, Cate Dicharry, and Katie Prout for enabling participation in Between the Lines, Book Wings, and Life of Discovery.

Thanks also to colleagues, friends, and family for their support of my work, particularly Sharon Achinstein, Connie Amoroso, Gina Apostol, James Arthur, Rick Barot, Charles Bernstein, Brittany Borghi, Nate and Thea Brown, Greg Alan Brownderville, Jerry Costanzo, Michael Dumanis, Tarfia Faizullah, Jim Galvin, Kevin A. González, Danny Khalastchi, Cynthia Lamb, Thalia Leaf, Joseph Harrison, Terrance Hayes, Brenda Hillman, Philip Hoy, Eleza and Hil Jaeger, Ilya Kaminsky, Kristin Kelly, Mark Levine, Jane Lewty, Emily and Harry Malech, Bill Manhire, Amy Margolis, Jean McGarry, Erika Meitner, Andrew Motion, Paul Muldoon, Caryl Pagel, Jodi Price, Mary Ruefle, Kyle Stine, Anne Savarese, Zach Savich, Harry Stecopoulos, Susan Stewart, Cole Swensen, Jan Weissmiller, Greg Williamson, Susan Wheeler, Stephen Yenser, David Yezzi, Dean Young, and the communities of the Iowa Youth Writing Project and Writers in Baltimore Schools.

And special thanks to Mary Jo Salter for her mentorship and editorial insights.

In memoriam Mark Bilbrey and Jason Bradford and Joe Crowley and Patrick Flynn Eckenrode and Kokoy F. Guevara and Erik Lemke and J. D. "Sandy" McClatchy and Jane Mead and Judd Hunter Phillips.